Original title:
Island Dreams and Ocean Whispers

Copyright © 2025 Creative Arts Management OÜ
All rights reserved.

Author: Tobias Winslow
ISBN HARDBACK: 978-1-80581-544-0
ISBN PAPERBACK: 978-1-80581-071-1
ISBN EBOOK: 978-1-80581-544-0

Enchantment Beneath the Celestial Sea

Beneath the stars, the seashells sing,
A crab in pants, doing its thing.
The jellyfish dance with graceful flair,
While dolphins giggle without a care.

The winds tell tales of clumsy ghouls,
Trying to surf on floating stools.
Seagulls squawk in a comical row,
As mermaids try on their best sun glow.

A fish in a tux gives a wink and a nod,
While octopuses play an outlandish fraud.
Each splash and bubble brings laughter anew,
With a seaweed party, oh what a view!

So raise a toast with a coconut cup,
To the silly creatures, let's giggle it up!
For in this realm where the waves gleam bright,
Every little mishap is pure delight!

Lull of the Gentle Swell

The waves roll in with a chuckle,
Seagulls dance, it's a silly shuffle.
Fish wear hats, they're quite the sight,
Sunbathers giggle, in pure delight.

Coconuts drop like surprise grenades,
Flip-flop warriors in sunlit parades.
The tide whispers jokes that are quite absurd,
As crabs throw parties, oh, how they stirred!

The Call of the Siren's Song

A mermaid sings with a voice so sweet,
But only invites folks with two left feet.
Sailors hear tunes that twirl their brain,
While mackerel dance like it's a train.

Shells jam-packed with gossip and cheer,
Tidal waves gossip, 'Oh, don't come near!'
For every sailor who tries to glide,
Is met with seaweed, their hair styled wide!

Daydreams Beneath the Palm

Beneath tall palms, thoughts float up high,
Where hammock swings can make you sigh.
A lizard in shades sips lemonade,
While flip-flops conquer, as late sun fades.

Sandy toes and ice cream trails,
Pineapple dance to a beat that sails.
Fruits in hand, they wobble and sway,
Chasing crabs at the end of the day!

Tranquil Shores of Forgotten Lore

Ancient tales in sandcastles dwell,
Where mermaids spin yarns, oh, what a spell!
An octopus plays the tambourine,
While sea turtles dream of old cuisine.

Fishermen brag of the catch that's grand,
But find only shoes left on the sand.
With each tide, laughter echoes anew,
As clams concoct stories to share with the crew!

Celestial Currents of Memory

On a boat made of waffles, we float,
Sipping lemonade from a banana boat.
Sock puppets steer while seagulls squawk,
A fish in a top hat steals our talk.

The sun wears sunglasses, oh so cool,
Dancing dolphins throw a beachside duel.
With every wave, a giggle erupts,
Making memories as laughter corrupts.

Palette of the Sky and Sea

Purple clams in polka-dot attire,
Sunsets painted by a fish with fire.
Turtles tap-dance on the sandy shore,
As jellybeans rain, who could ask for more?

A crab in a bowtie tells a tall tale,
While flamingos skateboard, never to fail.
Clouds shaped like bears, oh what a sight,
Ocean's a canvas, painted just right.

The Allure of Gull's Cry

Gulls gossip while munching on fries,
With cheeky grins and mischievous eyes.
They steal our snacks but share their tales,
Of swimming in soup and salad gales.

Waves tap dance as the sun starts to set,
Knocking on the door of a seafood jet.
A pelican swoops, asking for a snack,
While a starfish plays the maracas, all whack.

Sonnet of the Silken Sands

Sands like sugar, sweet and fine,
Where flip-flops waltz and shells entwine.
Mermaids laugh with pirate glee,
Leaving behind a bubbly spree.

Hammocks sway in the ocean breeze,
While crabs host dances with utmost ease.
A coconut falls; we duck and dive,
In this silly paradise, we come alive.

Harbor of Forgotten Wishes

In a harbor of socks and lost shoes,
A crab steals a sandwich, such curious views.
Seagulls debate on crumbs of delight,
While fish laugh at the seagull's flight.

The pirate's hat flaps, a sight quite absurd,
As it floats like a feather, it's truly unheard.
A mermaid with fins, all tangled in threads,
Sings lullabies to the fish in their beds.

Driftwood Dances at Dusk

Driftwood takes waltzes upon the soft sand,
While clams cheer them on, all eager and bland.
A jellyfish twirls in a shimmering gown,
And the sandy old crab just wears a frown.

As night blankets all with its starry embrace,
The starfish recites poems—oh! What a place!
The tide giggles loud, in salty allure,
While beach balls bounce, looking for a cure.

Celestial Tides and Lullabies

The moon sneezes softly, it's caught in the tide,
Where sea stars play twinkle, and sea cucumbers hide.
The dolphins are wearing their best silly hats,
As turtles debate on the best place for chats.

Shells sing their secrets in voices so sweet,
A clam playing drums on the barnacled beat.
The water woos dreams with its bubbly embrace,
While a crab takes a selfie, just in case!

Secrets of the Coral Cavern

In a cavern of coral, where fish take a stroll,
Lives a wise octopus with a marvelous role.
He juggles five pearls while reciting strange tales,
Oh, the fish giggle hard as he roams with his scales.

Anemones dance in their vibrant array,
While sea urchins grumble, they just want to play.
A lobster with glasses reads books upside down,
As an eel makes remarks—when's the next clown?

Secrets of the Trade Winds

Sailed on a banana boat, what a sight,
Chasing jellyfish, oh what a delight!
The parrot squawks tales, half true, half lie,
While sunburnt tourists give a crooked sigh.

Waves roll in like a laugh, oh so bold,
Shells talk back when the stories unfold.
Seagulls steal fries as they dive with glee,
Life's a beach party, come join with me!

Celestial Balmy Nights

Stars like confetti, the sky's wild show,
Dancing in flip-flops, just move to and fro.
Crabs join the conga, all the sea tunes,
While we eat coconut, aiming for the moons.

Under the palm trees, dreams start to sway,
With coconut drinks, we'll giggle away.
A moonlit limbo, what a sight to see,
Chasing our shadows, wild and free!

Serenade of the Salty Breeze

The winds sing ballads, tickling the toes,
Fish slap the surface, putting on shows.
Flip-flops get lost in the tide's bold dance,
While crabs wear sunglasses, taking a chance.

Waves giggle softly, secrets in foam,
Boys throw back jokes, making sandcastles roam.
Laughter erupts, it's a merry parade,
As the seagulls plot for a snack raid!

Echoes Beneath the Waves

Bubble-blowing fish with tiny big dreams,
Pelicans waddle, planning their schemes.
Turtles dive deep, with style and grace,
While dolphins laugh at our awkward race.

Sounds of the ocean, a quirky tune,
In flip-flops and shirts, we sway under the moon.
A porpoise jumps high, gets a round of applause,
As we enjoy sunsets, taking time to pause!

Mysteries on the Moonlit Shore

A crab in a tux, doing a jig,
Fish wearing hats, oh what a gig!
Shells tell secrets, they cannot keep,
Waves swap tales as the sea starts to creep.

Seagulls gossip of treasures galore,
With sunglasses on, they come to the shore.
A sea turtle thinks he's a rock and roll star,
While jellyfish float like they're in a car.

Octopus dances, with eight limbs in sync,
Sandcastles laughing, they start to rethink.
Clams play poker, no one can bluff,
At moonlit shores, silly is enough!

Footprints in the Sand

A duck in flip-flops, waddles with flair,
Leaves silly prints in the soft, warm air.
Sandals of starfish, they gossip and tease,
"Who wore it better?"—they giggle with ease.

A crab with a shovel, digging for gold,
Finds only a sock, oh that's getting old!
Footprints are sketches of moments we keep,
As laughter echoes, so simple, so deep.

Kids leap like dolphins, splash here and there,
While seagulls squawk, as if they're aware.
A flip and a splash, the day filled with cheer,
Every small footprint tells tales, my dear.

Whispers of the Tide's Embrace

The waves tell stories in a funny way,
Of a whale who thought he could dance ballet.
Anemones giggle, tickling the toes,
Of floating beach buckets, everyone's woes.

Tides bring a riddle, a puzzle at play,
Where's the fish who loves to do ballet?
Salty sea breezes sing songs of delight,
As crabs twist and turn in the soft moonlight.

A dolphin named Fred dreams of being a star,
While flying fish practice their leap from afar.
Each gentle whisper makes mischief abound,
As laughter on waves is the best kind of sound.

Crystalline Waters' Caress

Bubbles are giggles in blue, frothy seas,
Fish wear tuxedos; they dance with the breeze.
Coral reefs chuckle, all colors in sway,
As a sardine choir sings songs of the day.

A floating pineapple wears shades and a grin,
While starfish contemplate if they can swim in.
The dolphins are plotting a grand ocean spree,
With a mermaid DJ, how wild can it be?

Seashells all gossip about party plans,
With octopi chefs flipping cakes in their pans.
In crystalline waters, the laughter runs free,
For the ocean is where we all wish to be!

Breath of the Tide

The seagulls caw with glee,
Their fishy jokes—much too salty.
I slip on waves, oh what a ride,
Falling sideways like a clumsy tide.

Crabs scuttle in a dance,
Pinching toes as if in trance.
I shout, 'Hey, give me a break!'
They snap back, 'Not a chance to shake!'

Sandcastles rise, then meet their doom,
As waves rush by, they're gone too soon.
I wave goodbye, they wave right back,
With each splash, it's a tidal whack!

Floating on a rubber duck,
My sea legs feeling quite unstuck.
With laughter echoing through the bay,
I'm not quite sure I'm meant to stay!

And the Ocean Sang

The ocean hums a quirky tune,
While fish join in with quite the croon.
A dolphin darts, a splash of cheer,
Squirting water, it's the life I steer.

A jellyfish floats, a baffled ghost,
With tentacles waving, it's quite the boast.
I try to join with my own flair,
But all they do is stare and stare!

Starfish lounge, with no care at all,
In their laid-back way, they have a ball.
I ask them for a tip or two,
They simply grin, like 'Get a clue!'

Sunshine winks from high above,
Seagulls dance, push comes to shove.
With a surfboard under my feet,
I'll ride this wave and face defeat!

Hidden Sanctuaries of Serenity

In secret coves where laughter blooms,
And crabs play house in sandy rooms.
A hammock swings, a dreamy ride,
But first I'll nap, and then I'll glide.

Coconuts fall with a little thump,
I dodge the rain when they start to clump.
They roll away, like cheeky friends,
Who knew coconuts could break amends?

A parrot yells, "You've got no style!"
I wave back with a goofy smile.
"Your beak is bright, but I'm quite spry,"
He squawks again, "Oh me, oh my!"

The sun does set in hues so bright,
In twilight's arms, we stage delight.
With laughter echoing on the breeze,
We find our ease, just do as we please!

Mirage of the Everlasting Shore

A beach ball rolls, it's on the run,
Chasing waves, I had my fun.
But oh dear, where did it go?
Off to seek a sandy show!

My sun hat flies—a bold escape,
With seagulls cawing, it takes the tape.
"Catch it, quick!" I yell and shout,
But it's too late; the wind's got clout!

Shells like treasures, I collect and boast,
But they're empty homes for a lonely ghost.
I take a selfie, say, "What a find!"
But the crabs roll by, and I'm left blind!

As day gives way to velvet night,
The stars twinkle with pure delight.
With laughter trailing in my wake,
Here on this shore, there's nothing fake!

The Dance of Starry Skies

Under the moon, crabs waltz about,
Jellyfish juggle without a doubt.
A dolphin's giggle, a fishy grin,
The stars take bets on who'll win.

Flip-flops flinging, toes in the sand,
Seagulls squawking, quite ill-mannered and grand.
A starfish's dance? It's just a flop,
While the waves cheer on with a splash and pop.

Turtles breakdance, moving so slow,
Seaweed sways as if in a show.
Shells clap loudly, making a scene,
Even the rocks have a groove in between.

So join in the fun, let your worries flee,
Under these twinkling lights, we're frolicsome, you see.
With laughter so loud, we won't be discreet,
In this zany night where oddball dreams meet.

Serenades of Foam and Light

The surf sings songs of a fishy tale,
As shrimp don hats and dance without fail.
The sand's a stage for the clams' grand play,
With pearls as props in a comical display.

Octopuses share the latest trends,
While crabs join in, making silly bends.
The wave's soft giggle breaks all the rules,
As starfish play chess with the beach's fools.

Seagulls are cackling, high in the sky,
One dropped a sandwich, oh my, oh my!
With seaweed hats that shimmy and sway,
This ocean's cabaret is quite the buffet.

Under the sun, we'll shimmer and shine,
In this raucous scene, all troubles decline.
With laughter and foam, oh what a delight,
These silly serenades brighten the night.

Adventures in Mariner's Dream

A pirate parrot wears shades with style,
While sailors strut their stuff with a smile.
The treasure map is a riddle of jokes,
Leading to barrels topped with rubbery folks.

Mermaids are laughing, their tails all a-swish,
Concocting wild stories, quite hard to distinguish.
With every splash, the sea shouts with glee,
A tango of nonsense, come dance with me!

The captain's hiccup makes waves of delight,
As jelly squirt cannons shoot foam in flight.
With sea shanties sung in a laugh-filled tone,
Every adventure out here feels like home.

So grab your snorkel and join the parade,
Where every wacky turn feels like fate's blade.
With each silly mishap, we'll all just beam,
Living the life of a mariner's dream.

The Calm Before the Currents

The ocean's stillness hides a funny plot,
Where fish are napping, perhaps take a shot.
The porpoises slumber, dreaming of fries,
While crabs draft plans in their cozy disguise.

A turtle sneezes, and waves start to giggle,
The sea's gentle humor makes even shells wiggle.
Though calm now reigns over the cobalt sea,
There's a sense of mischief, just wait and see.

Seashells gossip, exchanging their news,
About a sock lost in deep ocean hues.
A tidal wave of laughter might soon abound,
As this calm is just a prelude profound.

So savor this peace, enjoy the light breeze,
For hilarity brews like a quirky tease.
With the wink of the tide, fun's just around,
In the depths of the sea, joy's easily found.

Where the Sun Kisses the Sea

On a beach of sand so fine,
Seagulls stealing bread in line.
Sunburned noses, laughter loud,
A crab walks by, feeling proud.

Dancing waves with silly splashes,
Flip-flops flying in mad dashes.
Sandy sandwiches, what a treat,
But the ants think it's a feast!

Coconuts with goofy straws,
Sipping drinks that get applause.
Sunscreen smears and sticky skin,
Everyone's in a goofy spin.

At sunset, skies turn into jam,
Laughter echoes, "Who needs a plan?"
We toast to fun with joyful cheers,
And surf the waves of silly fears.

Hushed Hymns of the Ocean's Heart

Waves whisper secrets, oh so bold,
Fish in tuxedos, stories told.
Mermaids chuckling, tails a-swish,
They call for help, "Oh, where's my dish?"

Seashells sing on sandy floors,
While crabs debate on ocean wars.
Turtles giggle as they race,
"Slow and steady wins the space!"

The plump old fish with glasses sits,
Scribbling tales of seaweed wits.
"Once I caught a wave so high,
It nearly sent me to the sky!"

In moonlit beams, the waters swirl,
With barnacles that twirl and twirl.
"Let's throw a dance under the moon!"
The ocean laughs, "We'll be there soon!"

Drift Away with the Sea's Embrace

Float on a boat made of dreams,
With fishy friends and silly schemes.
A dolphin dives, shouts, "Watch me glide!"
The octopus waves with arms open wide!

A sponge gives hugs, "Come, join the fun!"
Atop a wave, we're spinning, we run.
Seas hellos in funny tones,
As jellyfish dance in squishy zones.

A shark in shades claims the throne,
"King of Sea," he loudly moans.
But pufferfish blow up with glee,
"Hey dude, that crown looks good on me!"

With a wink, the tide rolls back,
"Next time, don't wear that bright plaid slack!"
A splash, a laugh, we drift away,
To dream of fishy tales and play!

Embers of Twilight on the Water's Edge

The sun dips low, painting the breeze,
Fireflies join for a night with ease.
"Did you see that wave's funny face?"
Laughing clouds share their space!

Campfires crackle, stories soar,
With marshmallow fights, who could ask for more?
A mermaid lost, "Where's my star?"
"It's under your fin, oh, how bizarre!"

Balloons float by, adorned with smiles,
As crabs dance Morris while we compile.
"Let's race to the moon!" one seagull claims,
Till a whale retorts, "I'll win the games!"

As starlit waves shimmer and glow,
We sit and giggle 'til dreams flow.
The ocean hums its jolly tune,
Chasing shadows beneath the moon.

The Song of the Seafoam

Bubbles dance above the tide,
As seagulls sing, they glide.
A crab joins in, tapping feet,
In a shell, a rhythm sweet.

The fish are laughing, swimming free,
In coral homes, they giggle with glee.
A starfish twirls, a seaweed twirl,
Creating waves in a salty whirl.

With jellyfish glows like disco lights,
The ocean parties through the nights.
Even the barnacles find their beat,
As the deep ocean shares its treat.

So let the waves, with voices loud,
Invite all sea critters, proud.
For every splash and foam-filled cheer,
The sea is a stage for all to hear!

A Canvas of Blue Horizons

The sky throws paint, shades so bright,
Brush strokes of laughter, pure delight.
Clouds parade like fluffy sheep,
While ocean giggles, secrets to keep.

The waves invite, 'Come take a dip!'
While dolphins play, they twist and flip.
A boat's hat flies, sails in a rush,
As fish jump up, causing a fuss.

Colors collide, in sunlit glee,
The horizon whispers, 'Dance with me!'
As beach balls bounce, kids make a splash,
In this funny game, all hopes clash.

So paint your world with ocean hues,
With laughter and waves, you'll never lose.
A canvas spread across the sea,
Where every breeze brings joy, so free!

The Compass of Heartbeats

A compass spins, all giddy and whirled,
Pointing to treasures beneath the world.
With goofy birds leading the way,
They squawk in rhythm, forever gay.

The seashells hum a quirky tune,
As fish form lines like a funky moon.
The octopus waves with all of its arms,
While crabs march by, with unusual charms.

Each heartbeat echoes a daring quest,
Where laughter floats and dreams manifest.
With a wink and a nudge, the sea invites,
To join the dance under twinkling lights.

So follow the compass, let laughter steer,
Through waves of joy, far and near.
In this whimsical realm of mirth,
Every heartbeat sings of joy and worth!

Sunlit Reflections Above the Abyss

Sunlight winks on the ocean's face,
While silly fish create a chase.
A shadow lurking, it's just a rug,
That flounder's dance is all a mug!

Squid ink tells stories, funny and wild,
Of jellyfish pranks, like a playful child.
Seashells chuckle, all lined up in rows,
As the tide spills secrets—who knows what flows?

The sun takes a bow, low in the west,
As seagulls screech, they're simply the best.
A laughter spills over, bright like the day,
Riding the waves, come join the play!

Each ripple and roar, a joke to embrace,
With joy in the air, let's pick up the pace.
In blue waters deep, with fun to persist,
The reflections of joy, with laughter, insist!

A Dance With the Siren's Song

Upon the shore, the mermaids sing,
With seashell hats, they dance and swing.
Their tails like ribbons, bright and bold,
They'll steal your heart, or so I'm told.

A fisherman stopped, dropped his net,
To join their jive, he soon did fret.
He tripped on sand, fell with a splash,
They giggled loud, oh, what a crash!

With frothy waves, they twirled about,
The sailor slipped, his boots flew out.
Flipping, flopping, in a whirl,
He yelled, "Please, teach me that twirl!"

Yet in the end, he danced alone,
With jellyfish as his new throne.
The mermaids winked, in water hid,
Laughing softly, "What a kid!"

Horizon's Lure

A seagull swoops, a crab gives chase,
They're racing fast, oh, what a race!
The sunbeam winks, a mischievous grin,
As the ocean waves toss them in.

With kites in tow, they sailed at sea,
Eating sandwiches with glee.
But one strong gust, the kites took flight,
And lunch flew off—what a silly sight!

The fish below laughed at this show,
While turtles swayed, going slow,
The horizon winked, "You're not so bright,"
As jellyfish jived in sheer delight!

"Next time, hold on!" a crab did shout,
But on the beach, fun was about.
With giggles loud and laughter sweet,
A quirky rhythm, a moving beat!

The Nautical Ballet

Under the waves, a ballet fine,
With dolphins dancing, a silly line.
They twirl and spin, in water's swell,
While seaweed sways—oh, what a spell!

A fish in a tutu, what a sight,
Flipping and flopping with sheer delight.
The octopus plays the piano tight,
While crabs clap claws, what a fun night!

A whale peeked in, gave a grand bow,
"Join our show, I can teach you how!"
But upon his leap, he missed the beat,
And landed smack—it was quite the feat!

Yet laughter echoed through the blue,
With every splash, the fun just grew.
The ocean's stage, a marvelous place,
Where silliness blooms, full of grace!

Whispers in the Coral Reef

In the coral garden, secrets swam,
Where fish wore glasses, quite the jam.
With bubbles popping, they made their way,
Whispering tales of the silliest day.

A clownfish chuckled, "Look at me!"
As he juggled shells, quite carefree.
A sea turtle yawned, "Time to nap,"
But then he twirled in a coral wrap!

"Ouch!" squeaked a starfish, "Watch your toes!"
As a friendly shrimp made quite the pose.
They laughed and played, in colors bright,
Creating giggles beneath the light.

So if you dive, oh, take a peek,
At the wonders that make fish squeak.
For in the deep, where laughter reigns,
Every joke swims with soft refrains!

Shoreline Reveries

In flip-flops I dance, on sand like a clown,
While seagulls judge me in their feathered gowns.
I build castles of dreams, yet they tumble down,
A tide's a tough critic, it wears the crown.

With snacks in my pocket, I waddle with glee,
The crabs hold a meeting, just plotting at sea.
They scuttle and chatter, all laughing at me,
Will I join their ranks? Oh, what a decree!

The waves sing their songs, I try to hum along,
But my pitch goes awry, a comical song.
The fish roll their eyes, what could possibly be wrong?
Just a human in chaos, where I don't belong!

But sunset arrives, turning blunders to art,
And I laugh as I roll in the sand as I start.
There's joy in the weird, a true work of heart,
In this sandy charade, I'm my own funny part.

Tides of Echoing Thoughts

The waves got my back, they carry my chat,
Each splash a reminder, I'm soaking wet!
A dolphin swims by, says, 'Hey, look at that!'
I tumble and giggle, where's my cool hat?

The seaweed ensnares my toes with a grip,
I wave to my friends, it turns into a trip.
Who knew ocean plants could be quite the snip?
They're plotting my downfall; I'm taking a dip!

A swimsuit so bright, I'm a walking delight,
My sunscreen's a slip, oh what a sight!
The crabs form a band, making music so light,
While I dance like a fool, in my own funky plight!

With each flopping wave, I ride on my dreams,
A sailor with snacks, and goofy ice creams.
As laughter rolls on, or so it all seems,
I'm the captain of humor, or so it redeems!

Serene Horizons Await

With a towel as cape, I soar through the breeze,
While shells debate loudly on their own strategies.
I sit by the shore, a lunch intersperses,
The gulls eye my fries, these feathered adversaries!

Beneath a bright sun, with laughter in hand,
The sand takes my shoes, oh isn't it grand?
I giggle at tides, they follow my command,
As I trip in my flip-flops, too goofy to stand!

Each wave brings a tale, of mishaps and glee,
A starfish gives thumbs up to my folly spree.
I ponder, the ocean's got secrets for me,
To find joy in the flubs, somehow, that's the key!

As dusk cloaks my antics, in pastel delight,
I gather my wits, the stars start a light.
With laughter, I conquer this shoreless night,
Each joke carried softly on waves, out of sight.

The Call of Distant Seas

Oh the rumble of laughter, like waves on the shore,
A coconut's grin gives me jokes to explore.
With sunburned cheeks, I've quite lost my decor,
As fishy friends giggle, I'm their personal lore!

The tides tell me stories, that tickle my heart,
Of pirates who stumble, a ridiculous start.
With treasure maps folded and boats built from art,
I laugh at their losses, oh where do I part?

Octopus in shades, he's got style and flair,
He struts through the sea, causing quite the stare.
I wave with my fries, but he doesn't care,
Just dances away with an elegant air!

Tomorrow I'll sail to horizons anew,
With dolphins as dancers and sunbeams in view.
A voyage of jokes, where laughter's the cue,
I'll cherish the sea and its antics, it's true!

Constellations of Coral Dreams

Beneath the waves, a fish named Fred,
Wears a top hat, he laughs instead.
Crabs in tuxedos dance with glee,
As jellyfish sing in harmony.

Turtles play chess, a game so grand,
With seashells for pieces, oh isn't it grand?
Starfish cheer loud, they're quite the crew,
With sea cucumbers serving fondue!

Octopus jokes with eight arms to spare,
Puffing up fish are caught unaware.
Clams tell tales of treasures untold,
While dolphins giggle, oh so bold!

Every splash brings laughter and cheer,
In this wild world, there's nothing to fear.
The sea's a circus, come join the fun,
Together we bask in the warm sun!

The Lull Before the Storm

A pelican perched, with a grin so wide,
Betting on fish, oh what a ride!
But seagulls squawk, 'Watch out below!
The waves might toss you, just so you know!'

Clouds gather round for a little gossip,
While crabs flip burgers on a tiny pitstop.
Fish in the deep keep looking for snacks,
As seaweed dancers practice whale hacks.

Then comes the breeze, a mischievous breeze,
Blowing hats off with such playful ease.
Shells start to jiggle, the sea starts to spin,
A pirate parrot shouts, "Let the fun begin!"

But just for a moment, let's take it slow,
For laughter and joy must surely flow.
So join the parade with your floaty and beam,
Before the chaos, embrace the dream!

Mosaic of Seashell Secrets

In a world of shells, a secret league,
With mermaids sipping on seaweed fatigue.
They trade tales of tides and sticky goo,
While clam shell carriages roll into view.

Starfish artists paint with salty strokes,
Creating masterpieces that make folks choke.
Crabs critique with their claws held tight,
Saying, "Not bad, but the angles aren't right!"

Seashells whisper with a gentle swirl,
Confessions shared in a watery whirl.
Dolphins giggle at the latest craze,
As barnacles brag in their awkward ways.

Each grain of sand holds stories galore,
While eels slide by wanting to roar.
In this peculiar place of aquatic design,
Laughter bubbles up, like a sparkling wine!

The Dawn Chorus of Coastal Hilltops

At dawn, the crabs hold a karaoke night,
With seagulls as judges, oh what a sight!
The shore is alive with chortles and cheers,
As barnacles sing with no sign of fears.

Pelicans flap, trying to find the key,
While fish in the waves hum their melody.
The sun peeks out, spreading golden rays,
Lighting up anchors lost in a daze.

Starfish do solos, elegant and bold,
While conch shells add a spin of old.
"I'm ready for the concert!" a clam starts to shout,
With his mates all yelling, "Turn it up, no doubt!"

So here on the coast, we'll dance through the day,
With waves as our rhythm, come join in the fray.
Each chuckle and song, with sea breeze in tow,
At dawn's lively show, let the laughter flow!

Celestial Harmony by the Shore

Beneath the waves, a crab sings songs,
With a voice that really doesn't belong.
Seagulls waltz in a dizzying spin,
While shells compete for who will win.

A starfish tried a limbo dance,
As fish clapped, giving it a chance.
The tide rolled in and swept them away,
Now they all laugh at that crazy day.

Seashells giggle in a pile,
Each one harboring its own style.
The surf bursts forth with playful grins,
Who knew that laughter washed up in fins?

The sandcastles laugh as they fall,
They tell each other that it's just a ball.
Coconuts chuckle in the moonlight beam,
What a riot, this oceanic dream!

Lost Notes of a Sea-Whispered Tale

A fish with glasses reads the news,
Telling turtles they've picked the blues.
An octopus took up the guitar,
His jamming sessions travel far.

The waves keep rhythm, soft and loud,
While crabs gather round, they're a rowdy crowd.
Clams tell jokes that end in a splash,
And dolphins glide by in a clever dash.

The tide hums tunes to sandy shores,
Shells echo back with silly roars.
Each current sways with such grace and glee,
Life here's a concert, come dance with me.

But wait! A seal joined in to sing,
Barking rhythms - oh, what joy they bring.
As the sun dips low, the laughter swells,
Who knew the sea held such funny tales?

Lighthouses and Starlight

A lighthouse shines with a goofy grin,
Lighting up paths for the fish to swim.
The moon sings softly, a lullaby bright,
Echoing sparkles in the cool, calm night.

Crabs build towers, oh what a sight,
While jellyfish juggle with all of their might.
Starlight twinkles like glittering bugs,
As the ocean winks and gives warm hugs.

Turtles slow dance to the ocean hum,
As seaweed sways, oh so much fun.
The light beams chuckle, guiding the way,
To seaside parties that last all day.

A wave crashes down, a comedian's jest,
The laughter rises, oh, they're truly blessed.
With each salty tear from laughter's tide,
They all celebrate the joy inside.

Treasures of the Tranquil Tide

Beneath the calm, a treasure chest waits,
Full of objects with hilarious fates.
A rubber duck and a lost flip-flop,
Giggling at stories, they never stop.

Starfish with hats, what a funky sight,
Pose for selfies, under moonlight.
Seagrass winks, teasing the shore,
While clams clap their shells, begging for more.

The tide chats softly, with secrets to share,
Of underwater laughter, that dances in air.
Sandy flip-flops are heroes of plays,
Bringing joy to all on those sun-soaked days.

A crab pulls pranks, a mischievous feat,
While keeping the beat with tap-tap feet.
The treasures of fun, in every wave rolled,
Make life by the shore a story retold.

Sands of Forgotten Time

In the sand, we found a shoe,
Who it belongs to, no one knew.
A crab danced in with a funny jig,
Claiming it's his—and he looks quite big!

Beneath the sun, we build a moat,
Our brave defense—a rubber boat.
Seagulls squawk and steal our fries,
While we plot our grand reprise!

A flip-flop fight ensues with glee,
As laughter floats across the sea.
Time ticks slow when you're all a-blur,
Dancing with fish and a wandering cur!

But as the sun begins to dip,
We find our hopes in hula hoop trips.
Grains of fun, so misaligned,
Who knew the shore had such a mind?

Celestial Coves at Twilight

The stars hang low, like goofy hats,
On waves that giggle, like silly chats.
A dolphin flips, takes a bow,
As we applaud, surprised—wow!

The moonlight dances, what a stir,
As crabs play tag, they hiss and purr.
Shells recite jokes, with seaweed punchlines,
Oh, listen closely—nature's timelines!

A jellyfish winks in electric glow,
Swaying with rhythm, putting on a show.
Fish in tuxedos swim and swirl,
In ocean balls, under seashell pearls!

So come, let your strangers be fun,
In waters where laughter's second to none.
We'll stroll the shore with grins so wide,
Under twilight gazes, as the tides provide.

Saltwater Serenades

Whispers of salt ride the breeze,
As crabs start dancing—if you please!
They twirl and spin in funny flocks,
While starfish line up as anchor rocks.

Seagulls croon in off-key ways,
They earn their tips with screeching praise!
Our flip-flops flap in perfect tune,
Creating music: the beach's boon!

With buckets in hand, we search for gold,
But find pop cans—what's the story told?
Treasure here is where laughter glows,
Amongst the waves, where silliness flows!

So join the song of salty cheer,
As tiny fish giggle in the clear.
We'll toast to tides and tickled feet,
In salty moments that can't be beat!

Waves of Memory Unfurl

The waves crash loud, a joyful cheer,
As memories bubble like frothy beer.
A sea turtle swims with a playful laugh,
While we slip and slide on the seaweed path.

Surfboards tumble, wipeouts galore,
As we tumble in heaps, yelling for more!
Fish give thumbs up, in their own way,
Saying, "Go ahead, brighten the day!"

Sandcastles rise like towers of glee,
With moats that splash, how fun can it be!
Our sea sponge buddy wears a crown,
While jellyfish float and dance around town!

So gather your friends, let's ride that tide,
In this whirling world, we'll joyfully glide.
With laughter in waves, our hearts will swell,
As memories unfurl in a comedy shell!

Whirling Dervishes of Seafoam

On a shore so bright and sunny,
Seagulls flap like they're all funny.
A crab dug in with a little dance,
Made a fool of me at first glance.

With a flip and a splash, he takes a bow,
Waving at shells, oh what a show!
For every wave, there's a giggle to share,
The ocean's laughter fills the air.

Swirling mist, a joyous spritz,
Salty tales of sandy wits.
Dancing tides do a merry jig,
While the sandcastles break, oh so big!

The sun sets low, a golden flair,
With silly seaweed stuck in my hair.
As moonlight twinkles on frothy glee,
I wave to the fish, "Laugh along with me!"

Tidal Passions and Ethereal Castaways

Oh, the fish wear suits, what a sight!
With top hats that glide in the moonlight.
The dolphins laugh and play with cheer,
Trying to catch a frisbee near.

Mermaids gossip in shiny shells,
Trading stories of ocean spells.
But when the octopus starts to dance,
I can't help but join, it's my last chance!

The starfish stares with fuzzy eyes,
Wondering just how deep this lies.
We twirl and swirl, a shimmery crew,
In a world where the silly feels brand new!

But as the night creeps, they start to tire,
Floating on pools of dreams and desire.
With a wink and a splash, they bid adieu,
To all the shenanigans, the laughs we knew!

Reverberations of the Deep Blue

Bubbles rise with a cheeky pop,
Echoing laughter, we just can't stop.
The sea turtles join in with a grin,
As a whale hums a tune, let the fun begin!

In underwater caves, the shrimp hold court,
Debating if crabs are just a sport.
But when the clownfish starts to tease,
We all dissolve into giggles with ease.

The seaweed swings, a party galore,
With anemones dancing right by the shore.
It's a raucous ball in the briny deep,
Where even the sea cucumbers leap!

As the sun dips low, the shadows sway,
Crabs crab-walk home at the end of the day.
With bubbles of laughter floating away,
The ocean hums soft, until the next play!

Pastel Calms Beneath the Waves

In hues of pink and lavender skies,
The fish sport shades, oh, what a surprise!
Bubbles blow out like candy dreams,
As they plot their next, silly schemes.

With jellyfish floating like chewy treats,
They dance 'round clams in their funny feats.
The colors whirl, in a vibrant spree,
We swim and giggle, just wait and see!

Seahorses strut in elegant shoes,
With a wink to the rays, it's time to amuse.
The sand dollars join in, oh my, what fun,
Chasing the tide until the day's done!

Then twilight brings a glittery glow,
With laughter echoing under the flow.
As stars twinkle above with a gleeful chime,
We drift off to sleep, dreaming of rhyme!

Morsels of the Mesmerizing Current

Fishing for snacks on a sunny spree,
A seagull swoops down, oh what a glee!
He steals my sandwich, it's quite a feat,
I chase him around with bare, wobbly feet.

The waves giggle softly, a bubbly delight,
As crabs make a dance, with pincers in sight.
Each splash is a chuckle, each tide a jest,
Who knew a beach could be such a quest?

Shadows of Palm Fronds and Dune

Palm fronds waving with a sassy flair,
They whisper secrets in the salty air.
The sandcastles wobble, like toddlers on a spree,
I wonder if they're as drunk as me!

Dunes like giants, with belly laughs akin,
To tumble down slopes in an awkward spin.
Oh, the sunburns I collect, they tell a tale,
Of daring adventures, and a beer-fueled sail.

Whimsies in a Seaside Town

A crab in a tux, oh what a sight,
He struts on the boardwalk, full of delight.
Next to a seagull with a top hat on,
They're planning a party from dusk until dawn!

The ice cream melts faster than time can fly,
While kids chase their dreams, and naps go awry.
With sand in my shoes and chocolate on my face,
I treasure these follies, this wild, joyful space.

Patchwork Skies and Sandy Shores

The sky's a quilt, stitched with cotton clouds,
As surfers ride waves, surrounded by crowds.
The sun's a jester with rays that poke,
While beach balls bounce like they're taking a joke.

A flip-flop flies, it's a battle of soles,
As laughter erupts from the moth-eaten shoals.
With sunscreen on noses, we squint at the view,
For life in this paradise is funny, it's true!

The Echoes of Lost Portals

I heard a parrot crack a joke,
As sailors danced with a mop,
The fish all chuckled in the brook,
While mermaids sang, 'Please, don't stop!'

A treasure map was upside down,
With X marking where I dropped my pie,
The map laughed back, 'You silly clown!'
And dolphins splashed as I asked, 'Why?'

A crab in spectacles told a tale,
Of seagulls knitting, wearing hats,
While jellyfish juggled in the gale,
And octopuses played with bats.

So if you hear those waves a-laugh,
Just know they're sharing all the fun,
In ocean's depths where jokes are daft,
And nothing's ever quite undone.

Ripples of Imagination

The waves were giggling, toss and turn,
As seahorses raced on a wild spree,
A treasure chest filled with candy churned,
While starfish painted the deep blue sea.

A giddy clam got trapped in soup,
Said, 'Help! I'm more than just a dish!'
While crabs performed a tap dance troupe,
Announcing, 'We are quite the swish!'

The sandy shores held beach ball fights,
As turtles wore sunglasses with grace,
And moonlight rose to spark up nights,
Encouraging all to join the race.

In dreamlike ripples that never cease,
Imagination thrives on the shore,
So come and play, it's a world of peace,
Where laughter echoes evermore.

Heartbeats in the Misty Surf

The ocean sighed, a heart so loud,
Telling fish tales with a wink,
While starfish twirled beneath a cloud,
And crabs served cookies by the sink.

Mermaids giggled, lost in song,
Flipping hair like fashion pros,
With seaweed crowns, they danced along,
While whales belly-laughed with flows.

The tides would bring the silliest treats,
As waves rolled in with squeaky sounds,
A conch shell whispered secrets sweet,
Causing dolphins to do clown bounds.

So when you hear the surf's light thrum,
Know joy is hiding in each spray,
From frothy whispers, laughter's hum,
Awake your heart, sail far away.

Cradle of the Seafoam

In the cradle of frothy waves,
A narwhal told of silly pranks,
While sea cucumbers danced like knaves,
In bubbles, they formed their jolly ranks.

The seaweed swayed in endless tease,
As fishies giggled, taking bets,
On which silly squid would fall with ease,
While a crab played bagpipes—no regrets.

A turtle tried to fly one day,
With seagulls laughing in delight,
But splashed in foam, he lost his way,
And joined the conga line at night.

So, come explore this giggling shore,
Where laughter dances with the tide,
In the cradle where silliness soars,
And all your worries can subside.

Sailing Through Celestial Tranquility

On a boat made of candy, I sail so bright,
With gummy bears crewed, oh what a sight!
The waves sing a tune, a sugary song,
While licorice dolphins dive right along.

Starfish play chess on the deck, what a game,
While marshmallow clouds float, never the same.
Turtles in tuxedos wriggle and grin,
In this sweet little world, we all just win.

The sun wears sunglasses, so cool on parade,
While jellybean rain falls, a colorful trade.
I sip lemonade made of fizzy delight,
And sail through the night on a cherry moonlight.

Oh, the seabreeze smells like peppermint dreams,
In my wacky boat life, nothing's as it seems.
With laughter and smiles, we ride every wave,
In this silly utopia, we all behave.

Fragments of a Coastal Dreamscape

Seagulls wearing hats, what a fashion show,
Flip-flops on fish as they dance to and fro.
The sand's made of popcorn, great for a snack,
While crabs in a conga line shimmy and clack.

Coconuts giggle, they roll on the beach,
And shells share their gossip, just within reach.
A wave of giggles swells higher and higher,
Sailing on surfboards of marshmallow fire.

The sun plays the drums, keeping time with the tide,
Mermaids sell ice cream; they serve it with pride.
A treasure map drawn with crayons and spritz,
Leads to buried snacks that were lost in the blitz.

In this world where the silly reigns supreme,
Laughter floats gently, like a whimsical dream.
With friends by my side, nothing could be better,
As we frolic and play in this coastal sweater.

Whispers of the Windswept Isle

Wind chimes and whispers drift sweet on the breeze,
Mangoes that giggle, hang high on the trees.
A parrot in pants tells a joke with a wink,
While octopuses argue on what sauce to drink.

Tide pools are theaters for crabs in a play,
With seaweed as curtains, they dance and they sway.
Each splash from the waves bursts with laughter so loud,
As jellyfish serenade, drawing a crowd.

Seashells exchange tales of faraway lands,
And flip-flops claim victory on sandy bands.
The sun sets in colors of strawberry jam,
While starfish applaud from their seat on the sand.

Oh, this whimsical place where the fun never stops,
Where laughter and joy bloom like candy-floss crops.
With oceanic giggles that bubble and burst,
We'll toast our adventures, in laughter we trust.

The Poetry of Pelagic Echoes

Underwater races keep fish in a flurry,
With seahorses speeding, oh, what a hurry!
The starfish play poker, while turtles just cheer,
And a walrus with glasses cracks jokes with good cheer.

Bubbles rise slowly, each one tells a tale,
Of seaweed that dances with grace in the gale.
The currents spell words in a language so sweet,
As they tickle the toes of the crabs on the beat.

A narwhal with style wears a bowtie so sleek,
While dolphins play harmonica, making us squeak.
Squid write their sonnets with ink made of dreams,
And whales sing in choirs, or so at it seems.

In a world full of laughter, let's sail and explore,
Each wave tells a secret worth listening for.
With joy in our hearts and the sea at our feet,
We'll spin tales of wonder and never retreat.

Journey to the Whispering Bay

A boat made of jelly, oh what a sight,
It bobbed in the waves, gave fish quite a fright.
With each little splash, we laughed so loud,
The captain wore sunglasses, looking quite proud.

We trolled for some treasure, found nothing but flotsam,
A sock and a shell, then we all just did blossom.
The gulls took our lunch, what cheeky little guys,
We waved sticks in anger, while covered in fries.

A crab stole the show, he danced with such flair,
In a tiny tuxedo, oh he didn't care.
We joined in the fun, with moves so absurd,
The fish cheered us on, though they spoke not a word.

As the sunset painted gold, our journey wrapped tight,
We laughed in the glow of the coming night.
With dreams full of jelly, and crabs in our heart,
We sailed back home, never wanting to part.

Marshmallow Clouds Over Aqua Depths

The clouds look so fluffy, like candy on high,
We wondered aloud, could we reach for a pie?
With giggles we bounced like the waves far below,
To catch a sweet treat, oh what a grand show!

Our boat made of cupcakes began to drift slow,
It soared through the sky like a marshmallow float.
Then came a dolphin, with a wink and a tail,
He serenaded us with a joke and a sail.

We sailed through the giggles, on jellybean waves,
A sprinkle of magic, our hearts it enslaves.
The wind whispered sweetly, "You're the best of the best,"
And we floated along, never needing to rest.

Oh, the starlit sky sprinkled sugar so bright,
We danced in our dreams till the morning's first light.
With clouds of the fluffiest marshmallow delight,
We smiled at the ocean, our hearts feeling light.

Notes of a Nautical Nomad

With a hat full of feathers, and fish in my bag,
I set up my camp on a bright ol' snag.
The seagulls all whispered, "You're doing it wrong!"
But I tapped my drum, and welcomed the throng.

A mermaid came by, to hear my sweet song,
She giggled and said, "You don't quite belong!"
With a wink and a splash, she showed me her game,
Making waves with the dolphins, oh what a claim!

We juggled the shells, and balanced on logs,
As turtles swam past, looking like old logs.
The crowd of the sea laughed and joined in the play,
A party was brewing, come night it would stay.

With silly sea creatures and laughter in tow,
I danced on the shore, with the tides in full flow.
For a life spent on waves sure is funny and bright,
I'm a nomad of waters, and this is my night.

Rhythms of the Rolling Sea

The tides tapped their feet, and the waves sang in tune,
They invited us over, to join in the swoon.
We strapped on our hats and jumped right in line,
With a boogie and grin, we felt so divine.

A crab led the charge with a two-step so slick,
The fish all partnered, their moves were real quick.
We waltzed with the waves, as the sun set so low,
The moon winked at us, "You're putting on quite a show!"

The dolphins played drums with the shells on the sand,
As the rhythm of ocean took hold of our hand.
We laughed till we cried, it was quite the big scene,
The sky turned a shade of hilarious green.

As the night rolled along with its tunes so absurd,
We danced on the waves, our hearts light as a bird.
With laughter and joy, let the ocean agree,
Life's much more fun with its silly esprit!

Beneath Canopies of Blue

Beneath the bright and silly skies,
A seagull stole my sandwich fries.
I chased it down the sandy lane,
While tourists laughed, they thought it plain.

In waters warm, with goofy glee,
A fish swam past, said, "Hey, it's me!"
It flipped and flopped, made quite a scene,
I couldn't help but smirk and lean.

A crab in shades danced on the beach,
Said, "Catch my moves, you'll learn, just reach!"
I tried to join, fell with a thud,
Now I'm the talk of the surf and mud.

Sunset came, we shared a laugh,
As jellyfish taught us how to dance.
With giggles echoing through the air,
Who knew the sea was so debonair?

Secrets of the Coral Depths

In coral caves where secrets hide,
I found a fish with quite the pride.
"I'm the king here!" it flaunted wide,
Until a sea turtle rolled and sighed.

A clam said, "Open up, and peek!"
But when I did, it made me squeak.
It shut right down, and with a glare,
I felt like I should just beware.

A dolphin jumped, in joy it leapt,
"These coral reefs, the fish you kept!"
But all the pretty fins I saw,
Just laughed at me, they knew the law.

We played charades with seaweed hats,
I tried to play catch with some clumsy bats.
But oh, what fun in this colorful mess,
In depths where laughter knows no stress!

Moonlit Reflections on the Sand

The moon was bright, a disco ball,
Reflecting on waves that start to crawl.
I practiced my moves, a bit of a show,
And tripped over a sandcastle, oh no!

Crabs cheered me on, with claws in cheer,
"Do the crab-walk, it's all clear!"
I jiggled about, made quite the splash,
They held their claws up in a dash.

A jellyfish floated in for a chat,
"You dance like the wind, but that's just a flat!"
We giggled together, under starlit skies,
Dreaming of midnight cake and pies.

The evening breeze whispered, "Keep it light,"
And so we danced till the break of night.
With tides and rhythm, who needs a band?
When moonlit reflections rule the land!

Driftwood Promises

A chunk of driftwood claimed its fame,
It told tall tales of the sea and game.
"I've traveled far, seen things galore!"
But really, dude, you're just by the shore.

With seashells gathered, we formed a crew,
Played hopscotch on waves, oh yes, it's true.
A crab referee called it a tie,
While starfish cheered, "You're both too shy!"

We made a pact, to never grow old,
In a world where silliness is gold.
So driftwood and I, we laughed all day,
While the tide tickled our worries away.

As the sun set low and laughter swirled,
I found bliss in the driftwood world.
With every wave, a new joke came,
In this sandy haven, I found my name!

Serenities of Salt and Solitude

Upon the shore, I build my throne,
A castle made of sand and foam.
The seagulls laugh, they steal my fries,
While I just watch with squinty eyes.

In tides that roll with slippery glee,
I find my hat has fled from me.
Chased by waves and frothy cheer,
It seems a fish might take it, dear!

With shells as plates and crabs as chefs,
I dine on snacks that nature left.
A starfish waves, a friendly hand,
While I declare my own food stand!

So here I nap beneath the sun,
With laughter loud, oh, what fun!
A sunburnt nose and toes in sand,
In this odd place, I make my stand.

The Lure of Distant Horizons

A boat I sailed on a zany breeze,
Waves bounced around like silly peas.
The compass spun with giggling charm,
We steered the ship, but caused alarm!

The fish below did dance and twirl,
While I just craved a swim and whirl.
With every splash, our laughter grew,
As jellyfish joined the hullabaloo.

In search of treasure, we dug and cried,
But found more sand than a treasure guide.
With eyes on the prize, we dreamed so bold,
And ended up with sunburns untold!

So raise a toast with coconut cups,
To ocean dreams that fill us up!
Though we may find ourselves quite lost,
It's the jolly journey that matters most!

Fables Beneath the Starry Canopy

Under stars that wink and sway,
I told a tale of fish at play.
They wore top hats with bits of sand,
And danced a jig upon the strand.

A crab declared he'd run for Mayor,
While seaweed served as campaign flair.
The clams all clapped, the dolphins cheered,
For a fishy leader they'd all revered!

The moonlit waves sang songs of cheer,
As we shared jokes and a cold root beer.
With shooting stars upon our toast,
We laughed until we felt quite lost.

Under the vast celestial dome,
In laughter's grip, we felt at home.
It's in the silliness we find,
The treasure that leaves less behind!

Windchimes of the Windward Coast

A breeze played tunes on shells so bright,
Making melodies with all its might.
The palms swayed gently, tapping along,
As crabs joined in and sang a song.

The sun blushed pink, in awe of the show,
While I tripped over my beach ball, oh no!
With laughter loud, I bounced right back,
To join the fiesta, not miss the snack!

The seagulls squawked a cheeky tune,
While clams did jive beneath the moon.
Lazy waves winked with glee in their rolls,
As everyone danced upon their shoals.

With windchimes made of laughter and fun,
Our spirits soared, we'd just begun.
In this silly world, we find our grace,
Where everything's a laugh in this sandy place!

www.ingramcontent.com/pod-product-compliance
Ingram Source LLC
Harrisburg PA
LVHW0125070526
810016B/1555